I Like Boxes

Illustrated by Stella Yang

I like boxes
and leaves.

NEW
500g

I like boxes
and shells.

I like boxes
and feathers.

I like boxes
and stones.

cat
FOOD
375g
NET
375g

I like boxes
and beans.

MILK

I like boxes
and flowers.

fresh
BOX
40
CLUB
22
SPECIAL
OFFER
38

MILK
Coconut
I like boxes and mud.
CHEESE RD.
COLA ST.

I
is
like
and
the
and
a